by K. C. Kelley

Minneapolis, Minnesota

Credits
Cover, © NASA Johnson Space Center/Wikimedia Commons; 4, © NASA/NASA Image and Video Library; 4–5, © Shaiith/Getty Images; 6, © Sjo/iStock; 7, © Nikada/iStock; 8, © Jurriaan Brobbel/Alamy Stock Photo; 9, © NASA/NASA Image and Video Library; 10, © NASA/NASA Image and Video Library; 11, © NASA/Wikimedia Commons; 12, © SpaceX/NASA Image and Video Library; 13, © NASA/Cory Huston/ NASA Image and Video Library; 14–15, © Steve Helber/AP Newsroom; 15, © J Marshall - Tribaleye Images/ Alamy Stock Photo; 16, © NSSDC/NASA/Wikimedia Commons; 17, © NASA/JPL-Caltech/Wikimedia Commons; 18, © NASA/Chris Meaney/Wikimedia Commons; 19, © Wilfredo Lee/AP Newsroom; 20, © NASA/JPL-Caltech/Wikimedia Commons; 21, © NASA Johnson Space Center/Wikimedia Commons; 22, © NASA, ESA, CSA, STScI, Webb ERO Production Team/Wikimedia Commons; 22–23, © NASA/ MSFC/David Higginbotham/Wikimedia Commons; 24, © ESO/M. Kornmesser/Wikimedia Commons; 25, © Marmaduke St. John/Alamy Stock Photo; 26, © NASA/Bill Stafford/Wikimedia Commons; 27, © NASA/ NASA Image and Video Library; 28TL, © NASA Kennedy Space Center / NASA/Glenn Benson/Wikimedia Commons; 28TR, © SAM/Wikimedia Commons; 28BL, © NASA/Wikimedia Commons; 28BR, © NASA/ Wikimedia Commons; 29, © lev radin/Alamy Stock Photo; 31, © little birdie/Shutterstock.

Bearport Publishing Company Product Development Team
Publisher: Jen Jenson; Director of Product Development: Spencer Brinker; Managing Editor: Allison Juda; Editor: Cole Nelson; Associate Editor: Naomi Reich; Associate Editor: Tiana Tran; Art Director: Colin O'Dea; Designer: Kim Jones; Designer: Kayla Eggert; Product Development Specialist: Owen Hamlin

Statement on Usage of Generative Artificial Intelligence
Bearport Publishing remains committed to publishing high-quality nonfiction books. Therefore, we restrict the use of generative AI to ensure accuracy of all text and visual components pertaining to a book's subject. See BearportPublishing.com for details.

Library of Congress Cataloging-in-Publication Data is available at www.loc.gov or upon request from the publisher.

ISBN: 979-8-892-650-6 (hardcover)
ISBN: 979-8-892-683-4 (ebook)

For more information, write to Bearport Publishing, 5357 Penn Avenue South, Minneapolis, MN 55419.

CONTENTS

OUT OF THIS WORLD!

People have been watching the stars for thousands of years. Many have wondered how to get to other planets or what the stars are made of. People with careers as scientists, engineers, astronauts, and analysts work hard every day to find answers to questions just like these. Whether riding in a rocket or looking deep into space with a telescope, there are jobs for everyone who loves space. It's time to reach for the stars!

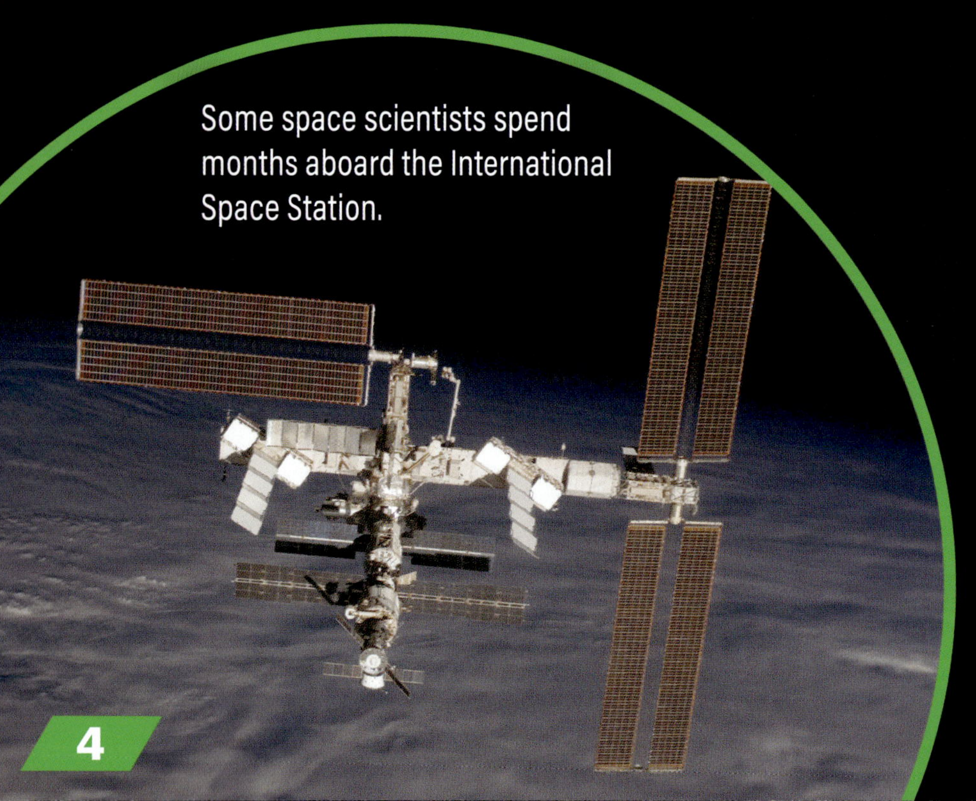

Some space scientists spend months aboard the International Space Station.

Many countries have their own space agencies. In the United States, NASA is the federal space agency. There are also some private companies exploring space.

STUDY THE STARS

Astrophysicist

Planets, stars, comets, galaxies, and even black holes—astrophysicists study them all. These scientists do experiments both on Earth and in space to learn about the universe. There are many kinds of astrophysicists. Cosmologists use information from huge telescopes to learn how the universe started. Stellar astrophysicists study how stars form and change.

What It Takes

- ☑ A math or physics degree
- ☑ An ability to work alone and with others
- ☑ Curiosity
- ☑ Creative thinking

Astrophysicists can predict when the northern lights will be visible by studying the sun.

Many astrophysicists also teach at universities or colleges.

Some astrophysicists **track** comets and other space objects that might get close to Earth.

SPACE TRAVELER

Pilot Astronaut

It's hard to get to space! Not only does it take a powerful rocket to launch a spacecraft from Earth, it also needs a skilled pilot to fly it. Pilot astronauts go through special training to fly spacecraft. They learn by flying planes around our planet first. Once in space, pilots work with **crews** on the ground to **navigate** in orbit or land their spacecraft safely back on Earth.

What It Takes

- ☑ Flight experience
- ☑ Leadership
- ☑ Navigation skills
- ☑ Computer skills
- ☑ An ability to stay calm under pressure

Jets on spacecraft allow pilots to change direction in space.

A pilot astronaut controls the speed and direction of the spacecraft from the cockpit.

Pilot astronauts need to log 1,000 flight hours in a jet before they can fly a spacecraft.

SCIENTIST IN SPACE

Mission Specialist

While some astronauts are pilots, others are mission specialists. The job of these astronauts is to run experiments and help **maintain** the spacecraft. Sometimes, they go on spacewalks outside the spacecraft to fix damaged equipment. They run experiments for growing plants in orbit, measuring starlight, or even studying how space affects the bodies of astronauts. Each experiment teaches us a little more about space.

What It Takes

- ☑ Physical fitness
- ☑ Willingness to live in close quarters
- ☑ Good hand-eye coordination
- ☑ An ability to work in low gravity

The longest spacewalk lasted almost nine hours.

Mission specialists are experts at doing experiments in the low gravity of space.

During spacewalks, mission specialists wear a special backpack with jets that allows them to **maneuver** around the space station.

COMMANDING THE COUNTDOWN

Launch Director

Three . . . two . . . one . . . LIFTOFF! Sending a rocket into space takes the work of many people. But only one person has the final say on when the rocket **launches**. The launch director is in charge of a group of scientists who plan for months. On the big day, the director's job is to get information from every person on the team to determine when it is safe to launch. Then, it's time for the final countdown.

What It Takes

- ✓ Communication skills
- ✓ Leadership
- ✓ Good decision-making
- ✓ An engineering degree

Hundreds of rockets are launched into space each year.

In 2016, Charlie Blackwell-Thompson (*pictured*) became the first female launch director for NASA.

The launch director has to watch the weather carefully to know if it's safe to launch a rocket.

IT'S ROCKET SCIENCE

Aerospace Engineer

Building a spacecraft that can safely carry people or machines into space is hard work. Aerospace engineers study for years to learn how to launch rockets safely. Some aerospace engineers **design** the huge rockets that push spacecraft to more than 17,000 miles per hour (27,000 kph)! Other engineers build the spacecraft that protect the people and machines on board.

What It Takes

- ☑ An engineering degree
- ☑ Teamwork
- ☑ Creative thinking
- ☑ Problem-solving skills
- ☑ Patience

Engineers build rockets of many sizes to send people, machines, and satellites into space.

Rockets that send astronauts to the moon are huge. Some are taller than the Statue of Liberty!

BUILDING SATELLITES

Satellite Engineer

Satellites are uncrewed spacecraft that orbit Earth. They perform tasks and gather **data** in the extreme conditions of space. Satellite engineers create satellites tough enough to work in extreme cold, strong sunlight, and low pressure. Some engineers have the job of improving the outsides of satellites to protect the delicate equipment inside. Others design cutting-edge satellite tools, such as **sensors** to measure light or heat.

What It Takes

- ☑ Knowledge of astronomy
- ☑ Problem-solving skills
- ☑ Computer programming skills
- ☑ Teamwork

In 1957, the Soviet Union launched the first human-made satellite, *Sputnik 1*.

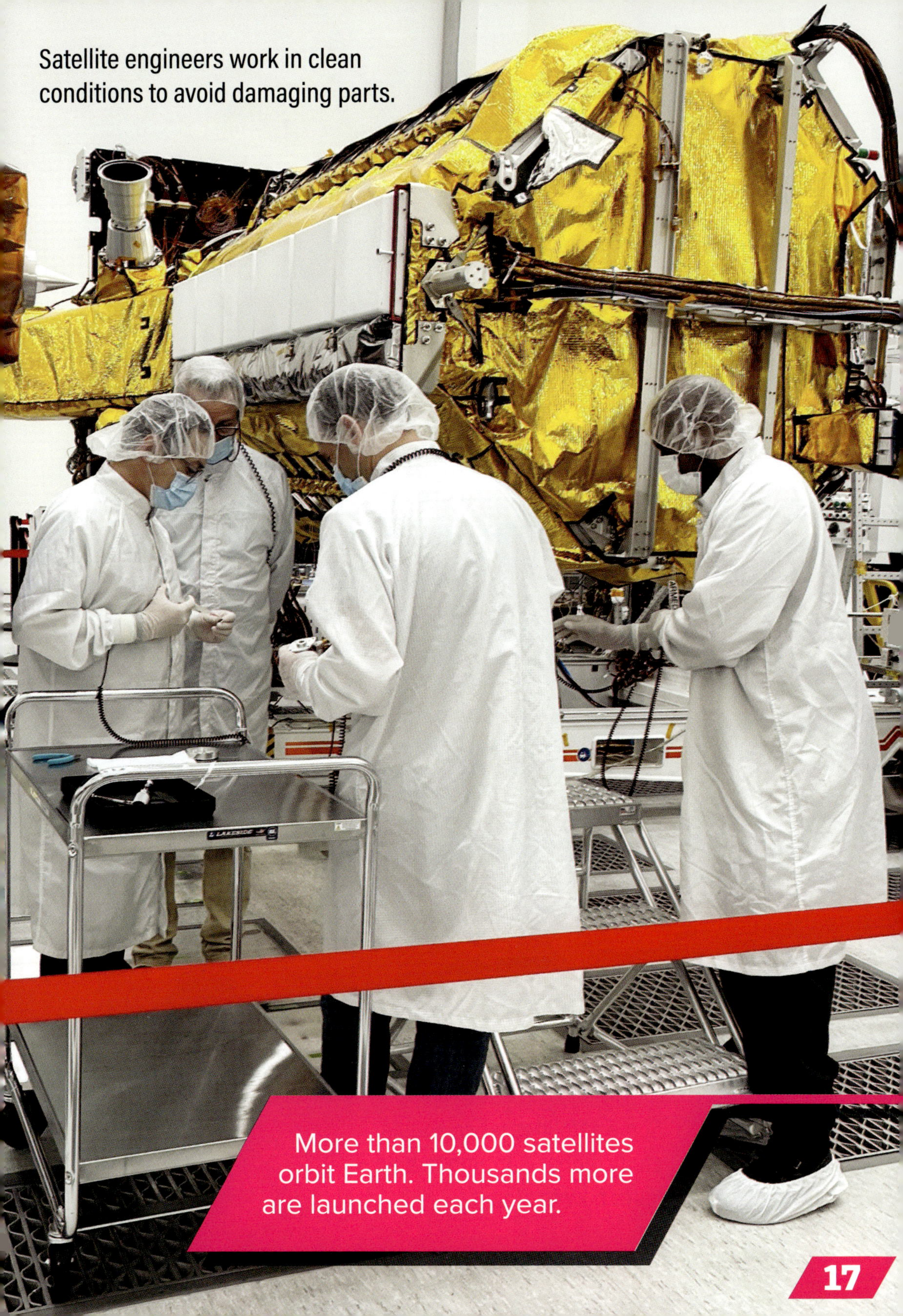

Satellite engineers work in clean conditions to avoid damaging parts.

More than 10,000 satellites orbit Earth. Thousands more are launched each year.

SPACE SPY

Geospatial Intelligence Analyst

Geospatial **intelligence** analysts use satellites to gain secret information, called intelligence. From this bird's-eye view above Earth, analysts are able to see what they might not be able to get close to on land. This gives them the ability to spy on other countries. They can use the information to protect their own country or learn how to attack someone else.

What It Takes

- ☑ An ability to sort through lots of data
- ☑ Knowledge of the world's countries and cultures
- ☑ A degree in history, geography, or science
- ☑ An ability to keep secrets!

Some satellites let scientists study global warming to help learn how to stop it.

Information from satellites is sent down to Earth for analysts to study.

Some satellites are powerful enough to see objects the size of a small car from hundreds of miles above Earth.

MACHINE HELPERS

Robot Designer

Robots in space can do things that may be too dangerous for people to attempt. Robot designers build and test machines that help astronauts do everything from recording experiments to moving **cargo**. Designers even build **rovers** to explore other planets. These wheeled robots take photos and rock samples to send back to Earth.

What It Takes

- ☑ A computer science, math, or engineering degree
- ☑ Problem-solving skills
- ☑ A love of machines
- ☑ Creativity

NASA's *Perseverance* rover is looking for signs of ancient life on Mars.

This astronaut is holding an Astrobee robot that uses fans to move around in low gravity.

The International Space Station has three Astrobee robots named Bumble, Honey, and Queen.

EYES IN THE SKY

Space Telescope Engineer

Space telescope engineers build the tools needed to study the universe. By putting telescopes into space, scientists can see things that would otherwise be blocked by Earth's **atmosphere**. Many of these telescopes use **lenses** or mirrors to focus light or other forms of energy onto equipment that can read the energy. Space telescope engineers are always working with other scientists to make better telescopes that can see even more faraway stars, planets, and other space objects.

What It Takes

- ☑ An engineering, astronomy, or physics degree
- ☑ Creative thinking
- ☑ Extreme attention to detail
- ☑ Teamwork

New telescopes can look farther into space than ever before.

The mirror on the James Webb Space Telescope is more than 21 feet (6.4 m) across.

Thousands of engineers worked on the James Webb Space Telescope, the largest space telescope ever made. It can see galaxies as far as 13 billion light-years away!

PLANET DETECTIVE

Exoplanet Researcher

Some space scientists study the planets beyond our solar system called exoplanets. Exoplanet researchers at NASA have used telescopes and other tools to find more than 5,000 of these distant bodies in the Milky Way galaxy alone. These researchers study what the exoplanets are made of, how they move in space, and whether they could support life.

What It Takes

- ☑ Knowledge of space conditions
- ☑ Teamwork
- ☑ Curiosity and creativity
- ☑ An astronomy or planetary science degree

The exoplanet Proxima Centauri B is slightly bigger than Earth.

The closest exoplanet to Earth is Proxima Centauri B. But it's still about 24 trillion miles (45 trillion km) away!

Scientists search for exoplanets by using telescopes and watching the movement of other nearby planets.

SPACE FARMER

Space Biologist

In the future, many more astronauts may live in space for months at a time. Or people may even live on bases on the moon or Mars. What will they eat? Space biologists are scientists with jobs studying how to grow plants in the low gravity of a spaceship or even on other worlds. They work in labs on Earth and aboard space stations to find which plants can best survive in space and on other planets.

What It Takes

- ☑ Knowledge of space environments
- ☑ Gardening skills
- ☑ Creative problem-solving
- ☑ A degree in biology or organic chemistry

Some space biologists practice growing plants in buildings similar to those that could be built on Mars.

This astronaut is growing radishes in space!

Scientists aboard the ISS have grown cabbage, lettuce, kale, and flowers.

LOOK TO THE STARS!

People who study or work in space are on the cutting edge of science. Every year, they discover new facts about our universe. These hard workers love to learn. Some even get to see their work flying by in the night sky. If you want to work in space, just look up! Is your future in the stars?

SPACE CAREER SPOTLIGHT

Victor Glover Jr.

In 2025, Victor Glover Jr. will lead the first mission to the moon since 1972. As a pilot astronaut, he will steer the *Orion* spacecraft close to the moon before returning to Earth. Glover and his crew will be in space for 10 days. At the end of the mission, Glover will be in charge of landing the spacecraft safely back on Earth.

GLOSSARY

atmosphere the gases surrounding a planet or moon

cargo a load of goods or supplies

crews teams of people who work together

data facts about something that can be used in calculating, reasoning, or planning

design to draw and plan how something will look and work

infrared light a form of energy that is similar to light but that can't be seen by the human eye

intelligence in war, information about a possible enemy or area

interference anything that gets in the way of something else

launch the rocket-fueled departure of a spacecraft from Earth

lenses clear curved pieces of material used to bend light to make an object look bigger

maintain to repair and preserve

maneuver to perform a difficult movement with skill

migration the movement of animals from one area to another at a certain time of year

navigate to find one's way from place to place

orbit the curved path of an object around a star, planet, or moon

rovers vehicles made for exploring the surface of a planet or moon

sensors devices that detect, measure, or record some kind of activity

track to follow the path or movements of an object

READ MORE

Dendy, Christina. *Astronauts (Extreme Scientists).* North Mankato, MN: North Star Editions, 2024

Owings, Lisa. *Aerospace Engineer (Careers in STEM).* Minneapolis: Bellwether, 2023.

Mattern, Joanne. *Amazing Space Tech (Design Marvels).* Mankato, MN: Black Rabbit, 2025.

Proudfit, Benjamin. *What Do Astronomers Do? (Careers In Science).* New York: PowerKids Press, 2022.

LEARN MORE ONLINE

1. Go to **FactSurfer.com** or scan the QR code below.
2. Enter "**Space Careers**" into the search box.
3. Click on the cover of this book to see a list of websites.

INDEX

ABOUT THE AUTHOR

K.C. Kelley has written more than 200 nonfiction books for kids. He has written about the International Space Station, spacesuits, and Neil Armstrong, among other space topics.